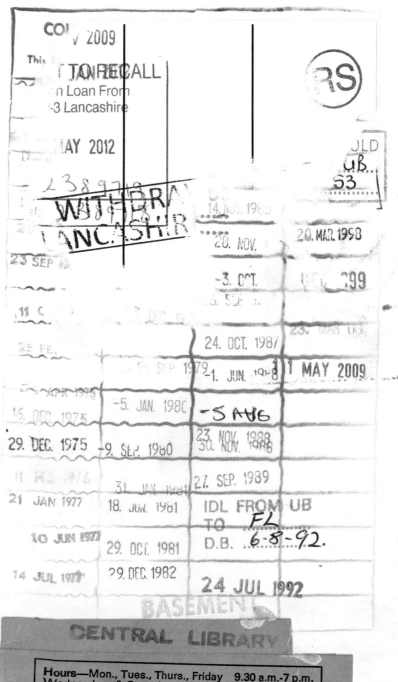

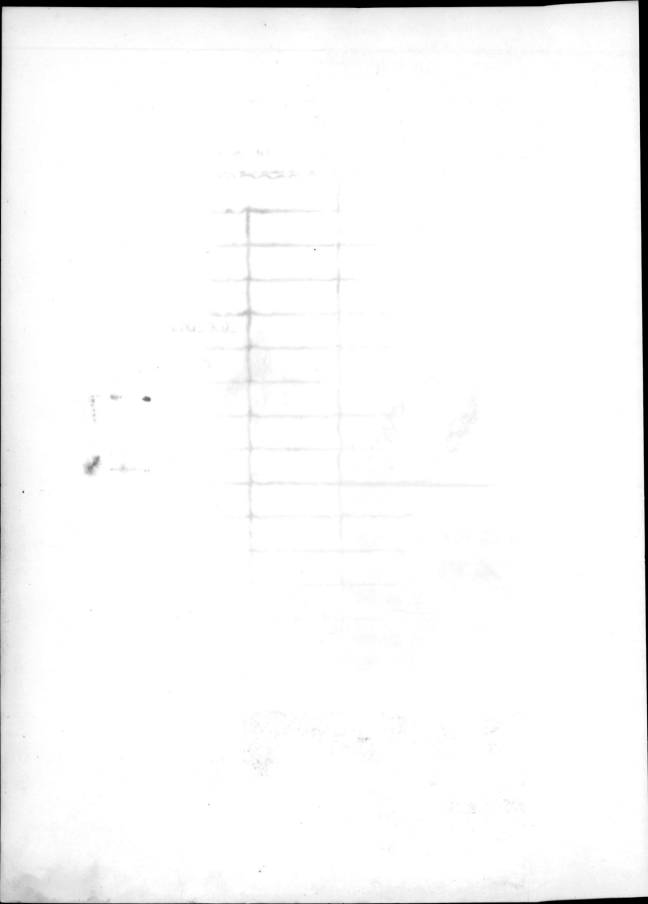

GREAT ENGINEERS AND THEIR WORKS

Thomas Telford

This portrait of Telford is the one he chose to be the frontispiece of his Atlas. *Published in 1831, it was engraved from the portrait painted by S. Lane for the Institution of Civil Engineers.*

GREAT ENGINEERS AND THEIR WORKS

Thomas Telford

Brian Bracegirdle BSc FRPS FIIP
Patricia H. Miles BSc ARPS

DAVID & CHARLES
Newton Abbot

Dedicated to

'TELFORD NEW TOWN'
In the hope that this famous name will be firmly perpetuated

Also by Brian Bracegirdle
Photography for Books and Reports

0 7153 5933 9

Filmset in Baskerville by Garland Graphics Limited and printed in Great Britain
by Biddles Limited Guildford for David & Charles (Holdings) Limited
South Devon House Newton Abbot Devon.

Contents

Preface

Thomas Telford was an engineer of stature at least as great as any before or since, although he is less well known nowadays than, for example, Brunel. The new town of Telford in Shropshire has been well named, for it was in that county that the young architect-engineer first showed his mastery of stone and iron in a way that advanced civil engineering techniques in what we would now call a breakthrough.

To follow in Telford's footsteps in Wales and the Scottish Highlands, to see the desolate nature of the country now and imagine what it must have been like when *he* travelled, can only increase one's appreciation of his works. His constitution, like many of his works, must have been of iron.

Less obviously, Telford's contributions to civil engineering did not stop at his actual works. It was to him that the system of contractors and precise specification is due–later to be developed as standard on railway construction. Telford was a canal and road man, largely because he did not think it right that the owner of a transport facility should be a monopolist contractor for its use which is inherent in the safe use of a railway. Well-called 'the colossus of roads' and 'Pontifex maximus', Telford's monuments are to be seen all over Britain in bridges large and small, in roads and in canals. It has been our great pleasure to follow his footsteps and to record his achievements. We are grateful to Aerofilms and Aero-pictorial Ltd for permission to use pictures 64 and 101, and to Neil Cossons for picture 40. All the others in the book have been made especially for it, though we have had to leave out very many others which deserved a place but would have made the book too long had they been included.

B.B.
P.H.M.

7

Introduction

Thomas Telford was born on 9 August 1757 in a remote valley at Glendinning, on the banks of the Megget Water above Langholm north of Carlisle. The exact site of the small cottage is now covered by conifers, but one can still stand by the water's edge and see much the same view as that of two hundred years ago. His father, John, died before the end of the year, and so it was that Thomas and his mother Janet moved to a cottage at the Crooks nearby; this remains although nowadays rather changed.

From these inauspicious beginnings, similar to those of many thousands of others, came one who was to be very different. Telford was to show the world new techniques in civil engineering, as we now call it. He was to work with his own hands with stone and iron; he said at the end of his life how great an advantage this had been. He was to establish guidelines for the organisation of engineering contracting, as considerable an advance in its way as any great aqueduct or road. Above all, he was to establish civil engineering as a definite profession, with its own scientific institution and procedures.

The area around Langholm has many memories of Thomas Telford. Apart from the site of his birthplace and the cottage at the Crooks, there are several products of his own handiwork with stone and chisels. The most moving is a headstone to his father in the graveyard at Westerkirk, and a more elaborate one to James Pasley of Craig. The young Telford, after a period working for neighbouring farmers, was first apprenticed to a stonemason at Lochmaben and then to another in Langholm–Andrew Thomson. Here his experience was extensive and valuable, for the local landowner was undertaking many improvements. A number of doorways

8

were made by Telford and are still to be seen, but the most important structure was the new bridge in Langholm, linking the old town with the New Town. This bridge still stands and under its western abutments, when the river is low in spring and summer, it is possible to see Telford's mason's mark–for he became a journeyman entitled to make his mark on his works.

While working in Langholm, Telford also discovered the joys of English literature. Miss Pasley, related to the Pasleys of Craig, lent him books from her own library and ever afterwards Telford was an avid reader and indeed poet in his own right.

Telford left Eskdale in 1780, having exhausted the challenges of his native valley. He went to Edinburgh and stayed two years, working on the New Town and Princes Street areas. He returned briefly to the Crooks at the end of 1781 when he was 25 and then, in 1782, set off on the long journey to London to take up work at Somerset House.

2. THE MEGGAT WATER (75/NY 297946–7 miles north-west of Langholm). *Looking down the valley towards the Esk, the site of Telford's birthplace is just to the right of the camera position where, in the middle of the young fir trees, can still be seen a large ash tree marking the few stones remaining of the shepherd's cottage.*

3. COTTAGE AT THE CROOKS (75/NY 296927–7 miles north-west of Langholm). *Originally, the central window was the entrance door, and there was a chimney at each end. Janet Telford and her son occupied one end during the years Thomas spent at school in Westerkirk and as a mason in Langholm. His mother stayed here for the rest of her life.*

While in London, Telford worked on Somerset House. This brought him into contact with eminent architects such as Robert Adam and Sir William Chambers. He very soon showed his skill and was promoted to be first-class mason, and worked primarily on the south-west corner of the building. A scheme to set himself and another mason up in business failed for lack of funds, but Telford did some work for William Pulteney, who was altering Westerhall near Langholm. Telford's work here evidently impressed the man who was to become the wealthiest commoner in England, and the two became friends. It was a friendship which was to have lasting importance for Telford.

4. (right) LANGHOLM BRIDGE (76/NY 363848–in Langholm). *The mason's mark adopted by Thomas Telford when he became a journeyman stone-mason. A number of these marks can still be seen on the western abutments and under the arch of this bridge. Each is about four inches high, and each was put there by Telford himself.*

5. (below) *The bridge itself, built about 1778, still stands as firmly as it ever did, in spite of the considerable floods which sweep down the river each winter. The photograph was made in summer when the river was low. A previous visit to look for the mason's marks (under the nearer side in this view) coincided with the water reaching almost to the bases of the arches!*

6. (above left) JOHN TELFORD'S HEADSTONE (In Westerkirk graveyard, 75/NY 313903–5 miles north-west of Langholm). *Cut by Thomas Telford's own hands as soon as he was skilled in working stone, this is a poignant memorial of son as well as father.*

7. (above right) THE PASLEY MEMORIAL (ten yards away from John Telford's stone). *Originally in the old church at Westerkirk, this memorial has been re-erected in the wall of the graveyard across the road from the church. The fine lettering is strongly reminiscent of that cut for his father's stone.*

8. (opposite: above left) DOORWAY IN LANGHOLM (by the side of Langholm library, 76/NY 365845). *Made by Telford while occupied as an apprentice in Langholm.*

9. (opposite: above right) SOMERSET HOUSE, LONDON (at the north side of Waterloo Bridge). *The south-west corner, shown here, was the part worked on by Telford, between 1782 and 1784.*

10. (opposite: below) COMMISSIONER'S HOUSE, PORTSMOUTH NAVAL DOCKYARD (181/SU 6401, but not normally accessible to the public). *Telford was here not employed as a mere stonemason, but as resident superintendent. This work lasted from 1784 to 1786, and the plan of the building is shown to emphasise the considerable increase in status and responsibility which Telford had achieved by the age of 27. He was already marked as a man of mettle.*

12

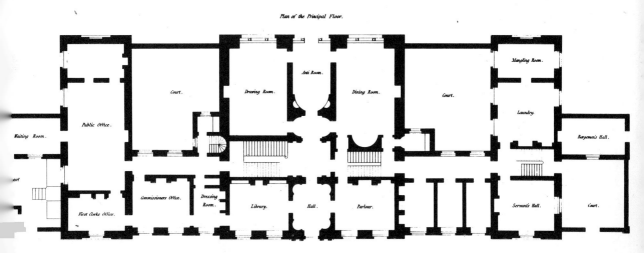

Plan of the Principal Floor.

Waiting Room.

Public Office.

Court.

Drawing Room.

Anti Room.

Dining Room.

Court.

Mangling Room.

Laundry.

Bargemen's Hall.

Court.

First Clerks Office.

Commissioners Office.

Dressing Room.

Library.

Hall.

Parlour.

Servants Hall.

Court.

Shrewsbury Days

William Pulteney had been elected MP for Shrewsbury, and employed Telford to make habitable the derelict castle, part of his estates. In 1786 Telford started the renovation, and by the start of 1787 had also been appointed Surveyor of Public Works for the County of Salop. Pulteney had given Telford a great opportunity to make a name for himself, and this opportunity was eagerly seized. At this time engineering was hardly a profession, although Brindley had built canals and Smeaton a variety of works. Architecture was the career which Telford saw for himself, and it was initially towards this goal that he worked in Shrewsbury.

11. SHREWSBURY CASTLE (118/SJ 495128, in the centre of Shrewsbury). *Although an ancient and important fortress, the castle had suffered badly from neglect and active dismemberment until Telford started the restoration in 1786. Much of his work can still be seen in this main block and other parts.*

12. SHREWSBURY GAOL (118/SJ 496129, behind the railway station in the centre of Shrewsbury). *Plans for the gaol were originally prepared by J. H. Haycock, but they were much altered and improved by Telford. John Howard, the prison reformer, visited Shrewsbury in 1788, and was instrumental in suggesting improvements to the young Telford. The bust visible over the entrance is that of Howard, and the whole appearance of the buildings remains graceful. The work was done between 1787 and 1793.*

Telford worked on the infirmary as well as the gaol in Shrewsbury, and employed convict labour to excavate the Roman city of Uriconium. He made something of a name for himself by his advice to the churchwardens of St Chad's church. Called in to examine the roof for repairs, he found that the walls were unsafe and advised that they be repaired before the roof. His report was dismissed with ridicule; three days later the tower completely collapsed!

15

13. (above) ST MARY'S, BRIDGNORTH (130/SO 717928, in the High Street, Bridgnorth). *Telford designed few churches in Salop and those he did work on are simple but by no means unpleasing. St Mary's was put at the top of the High Street in Bridgnorth, and Telford must have had an eye for its overall effect, for the houses were there before the church. The whole building is seen to advantage from below, by the river, and it was his intention in design to avoid an orthodox chancel and nave so as to stress the undivided nature of the church and secure maximum audibility. The church was designed in 1792.*

14. (opposite: above) ST MICHAEL'S, MADELEY (119/SJ 696041, near the centre of Madeley). *Telford designed and supervised the building of this octagonal church between 1792 and 1796 (the chancel, deliberately obscured in the picture, was added in 1910). The square west tower has an arched entrance and the whole is both interesting and unusual.*

15. (opposite: below) *Inside, the east window in the later chancel represents the original window. The interior is not octagonal, but oblong–the vestries cutting off two triangles. The galleries are supported by columns, with somewhat Adamish appearance above.*

16

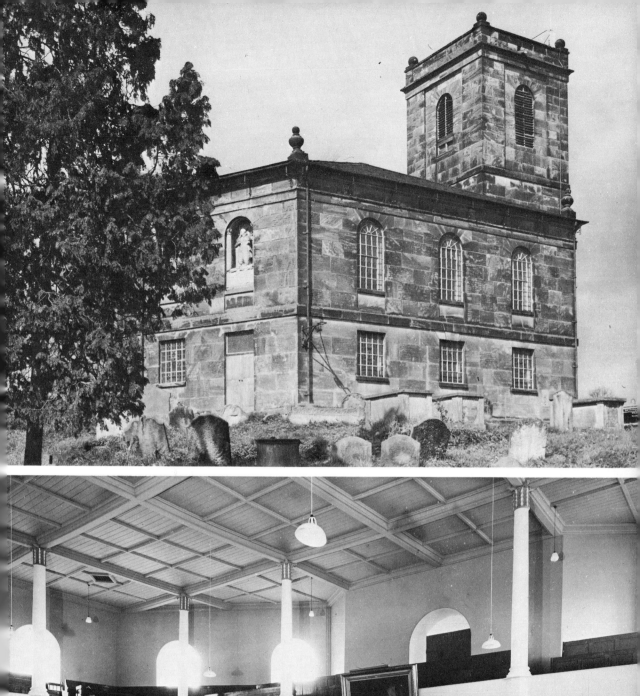

While working in Salop, Telford built over forty bridges in the years between 1790–96. Very severe storms in the winter of 1795 brought much work of this kind, for many bridges were washed away.

16. MONTFORD BRIDGE (118/SJ 432153–7 miles west of Shrewsbury, on the A5). *This is the first bridge to be built from Telford's own designs, from stone quarried at Nesscliffe between 1790 and 1792. He sent to Langholm for Matthew Davidson to superintend its building, starting a lifelong business association between the two. The bridge still carries the A5 traffic and has been widened to carry footpaths extra to the original width. The photograph shows the original masonry and the extra footways.*

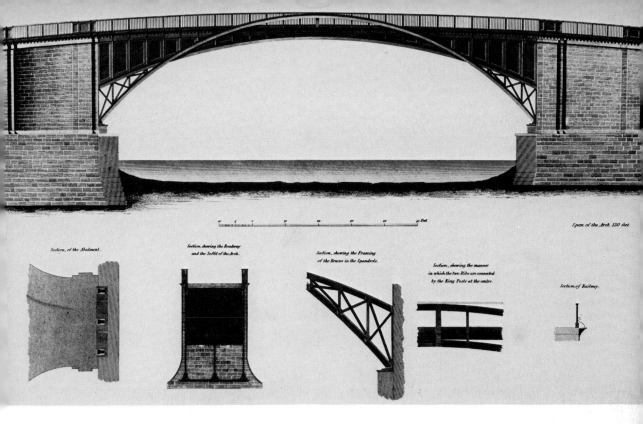

Section of the Abutment.

Section, shewing the Roadway and the Soffit of the Arch.

Section, shewing the Framing of the Braces in the Spandrels.

Section, shewing the manner in which the two Ribs are connected by the King Posts at the centre.

Section of Railway.

Span of the Arch 130 feet

17. BUILDWAS BRIDGE, *designed in 1795, has now been replaced and is shown as it appeared in Telford's* Atlas. *Two miles upstream from the famous Iron Bridge of Abraham Darby III, Telford's cast iron bridge at Buildwas spanned 130 ft. This is more than 30 ft wider than the Darby bridge, but the weight was only half that of the earlier structure. Telford was able to use a single span of flat profile, which resisted the tendency of the abutments to slide inwards and compress the arch. This early involvement with cast iron was to stand Telford in good stead for much later work with this material.*

Telford's work in and around Shrewsbury was much admired, and gave him great advantage when engineers were needed for major projects in the vicinity. Two of these were canal engineering works, one of them (the Ellesmere Canal) of considerable magnitude.

18. (opposite) GUILLOTINE GATE, SHREWSBURY CANAL (119/SJ 644153–2 miles north of Wellington). *The Shrewsbury Canal Company was authorised in 1793 to cut 17 miles of canal between Trench and Shrewsbury; William Clowes was the engineer. Clowes died, and Telford was appointed to succeed him in early 1795. Although a short canal and long derelict, the engineering features remaining include a tunnel, a very important aqueduct and some interesting locks.*

19. (above) *The locks have small clapper gates at their tops, as usual, but rather unusual guillotine gates for their lower gates. The original design is shown in these two pictures, with the vertically-rising gate counterbalanced by a box full of stones. The operating mechanism is shown clearly in this example, which is the one remaining in best order. There are several other such gates at the Wellington end of the canal, more accessible than this particular specimen.*

21

20. LATER GUILLOTINE GATE (119/SJ 674131–2 miles north-east of Wellington). *The earlier pattern was modified in some locks by the addition of a counterweight pit by the side of the overhead gear. In the background of the picture can be seen an earlier example with counterweight box over the waterway. This later example used a cast iron weight to the side of the waterway.*

21.   BERWICK TUNNEL PORTAL (118/SJ 538115–1½ miles north of Atcham). *Opened in 1797, the tunnel originally had a towpath, which was later removed to give the appearance shown in the picture. The portal still remains, but has been very recently bricked up. Although small, the masonry has a classic simplicity and beauty, its belling out making the tunnel appear larger in diameter than it really is.*

22. LONGDON-ON-TERN AQUEDUCT ABUTMENTS (118/SJ 617156–4 miles north-west of Wellington). *William Clowes had designed a conventional masonry aqueduct here; the workings were swept away by floods and Telford erected an aqueduct of cast iron instead. A few months earlier a much smaller iron trough aqueduct had been erected in Derby, but this aqueduct at Longdon is certainly the first substantial cast iron aqueduct in the world and a monument of the first importance. It is to be restored by the Ironbridge Gorge Museum Trust. The photograph shows the abutments, obviously reused from the completely different earlier masonry design. It may well be that the entire aqueduct would have resembled the two arches seen here, for that was the kind of aqueduct being built at that time. The masonry inserted at the ends of the brickwork is typical of Telford, and seems to represent his chopping off of the original structure to insert his own much smaller span seen on the left of the picture.*

24

23. *The aqueduct main span is shown here, with the other abutments across the Tern (partially in flood in this picture). The contrast between the wide abutments of the early masonry design, and the very narrow and economical iron trough with its airy supports is most marked. Telford had been appointed resident engineer to the Ellesmere canal before his appointment to this Shrewsbury canal, and there seems no doubt that this Longdon aqueduct helped to convince the larger Company that an iron trough was practicable at Pontcysyllte.*

25

24. (opposite: above) *This detail of the aqueduct shows the iron trough (long since dewatered), with the towpath slung alongside. The general arrangement of the sections is plain, and when bolted together all would pull tight. The ironwork is all original and in quite good order still.*

25. (opposite: below) *The trough commences with a brick channel, possibly part of the original aqueduct of masonry. This also is in good condition, and the original cast iron rubbing strips are still in place.*

26. (this page) *The detail of the pier support shows the relatively massive nature of the bases, and the cruciform section of the uprights combining economy of material with the necessary strength. The uprights are luted into slots on the base, which is also ribbed to withstand the considerable force of the river when in flood. Obviously, even at this early stage Telford had established the basic properties of this material, although it was only ten years before that he had been a mere journeyman stonemason. Telford was most fortunate to be employed by notable ironmasters, in a county where iron was of the greatest importance and an everyday material.*

The Ellesmere Canal

In 1793 Telford became resident engineer to the Ellesmere Canal Company. It was his achievements with this company which established him as an eminent engineer of his day–Chirk and Pontcysyllte remain as some of the most impressive monuments of canal engineering ever to have been built.

27. DRAWBRIDGE ON THE PREES BRANCH (118/SJ 492346– 4 miles north of Wem). *The Dutch-like appearance of these bridges, still numerous on the present Llangollen Canal, is typical of this waterway's functional approach. There is no need for expensive approach embankments, as the bridge crosses the canal only a few inches above water level. The stone-filled balance box ensures easy operation, and the small amount of materials needed for such a bridge ensures that the many accommodation bridges required on a navigation would be cheap.*

28. ELLESMERE CANAL COMPANY'S OFFICES (118/SJ 401343–
1 mile south of Ellesmere). *A group of Ellesmere businessmen promoted this
canal, although it remained isolated from the rest of the system for many years.
William Jessop was the consulting engineer, and Telford was fortunate in this,
for Jessop was a man of great experience but retiring nature. Undoubtedly,
Telford learned a great deal from the older man; the Canal Company was
fortunate indeed to have in its service two such engineers, for there were many
difficulties to be overcome. It was with the acceptance of the appointment as
'General Agent, Surveyor, Engineer' to the Ellesmere company that Telford
decided to commit himself to civil engineering, and not pursue architecture in the
future. By 1795 the canal from Ellesmere Port to Chester was open, and earning
a good revenue to be put towards the much more difficult construction to the
west.*

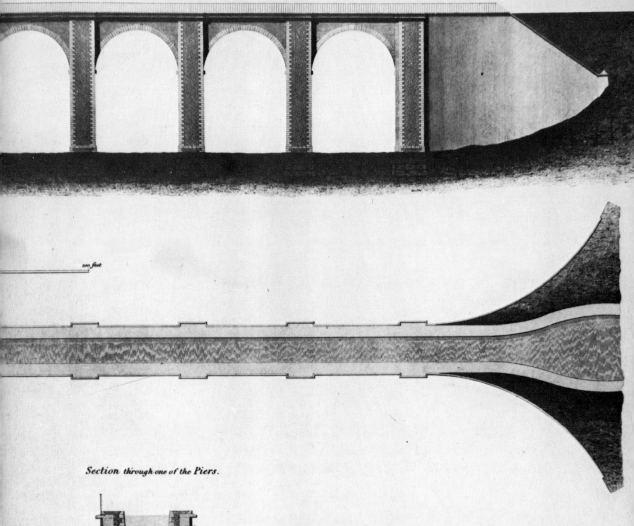

200 feet

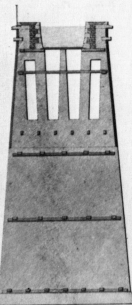

Section through one of the Piers.

29. (opposite) CHIRK AQUEDUCT (118/SJ 287373, just south of Chirk). *One of the major difficulties was to get the canal across the valley of the Ceiriog. The result was the aqueduct of ten spans each of forty feet carrying the canal seventy feet above the river. At first sight the aqueduct much more closely resembles a road bridge or railway viaduct, for there is little depth of masonry above the piers. The drawing from Telford's* Atlas *(29) shows how this was achieved. To save the great weight of the masonry floor with attendant puddling, Telford built the bottom of the water channel of cast iron plates. This reduced the weight and acted as a continuous tie to keep together the masonry walls under the pressure of the water tending to force them apart as in any aqueduct.*

30. (this page) *Telford's original iron railings are still in position above the slender masonry of the piers, dating from 1796.*

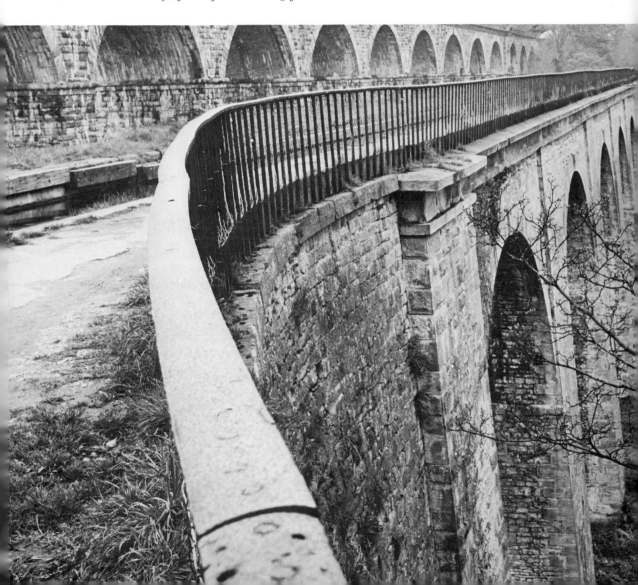

31. CHIRK AQUEDUCT *seen from water level, with the tunnel in the distance. On the left is the later railway viaduct.*

The ashlar masonry forming the sides of the waterway is backed by brickwork set in Parker's cement. The tops of the piers and the spandrels of the arches are made hollow, with interior cross walls. The cast iron bed plates for the aqueduct were supplied by William Hazeldine of Plas Kynaston foundry, near the further end of the aqueduct at Pontcysyllte; the contract was secured in November 1799.

The tunnel at Chirk incorporated another feature–a towpath. Although this seems an obvious feature nowadays, frequently boats had to be taken through tunnels either by shafting or by legging–pushing like a punt or walking with the legs along the tunnel lining while lying on the boat. Both were exhausting and inefficient, and the tunnels on the Ellesmere Canal were doubtless a great boon to the boatmen.

32. CHIRK TUNNEL—SOUTH PORTAL (118/SJ 286374, at the Chirk side of the aqueduct). *The tunnel is wide enough for only one boat at once, but as it is only a quarter of a mile long this was no serious disadvantage in practice. The original towpath is still in position, and the whole structure remains in good order.*

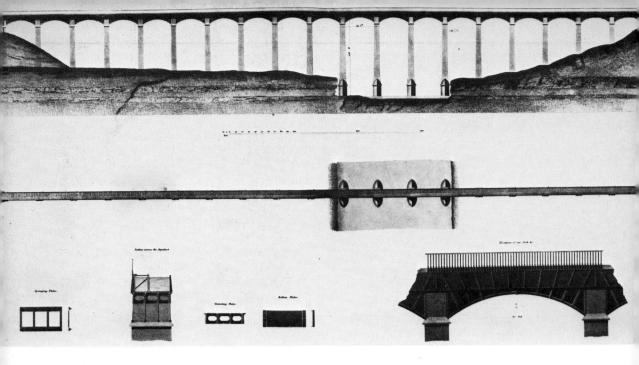

33. (above) PONTCYSYLLTE AQUEDUCT *from Telford's* Atlas.
*Without doubt, this aqueduct is the most impressive example of canal engineering
of its time. 1,007 ft long, and 127 ft above the river Dee, this aqueduct makes an
awe-inspiring sight, especially when standing underneath it. Such a structure
could not have been built conventionally of masonry, for the weight of the usual
puddled waterway would have required supporting piers of so great a section
that they could not have been afforded. The work was begun on 25 July 1795,
and the aqueduct opened in 1805. The earth embankments at the approaches
to the aqueduct were the greatest earthworks raised to that time, being 97 ft high
at the southern end, and a very impressive feat in themselves. The piers are
hollow with cross walls from seventy feet upwards, saving more unnecessary
weight, and the quality of the masonry is of the highest.*

    *The iron trough was cast and erected by William Hazeldine, and remains in
good condition to this day.*

34. (opposite) PONTCYSYLLTE FROM BELOW (camera position
117/SJ 271419, near the cricket field on the bank of the river). *The piers,
seen here from about one third their height, are most impressive as they soar
upwards to the iron trough. The great economy of materials is notable. At the
base of the nearer pier is the commemorative plaque which records the dates of
construction and the names of those associated with it.*

34

35. PONTCYSYLLTE FROM ABOVE (camera position 117/SJ 272422, across the canal from the boatyard). *The construction of the trough is seen here, and its brackets to the piers. All the ironwork is the original.*

36

36. PONTCYSYLLTE–NORTHERN ABUTMENT (camera position 117/SJ 272422, just below that for plate 35). *The masonry was built by John Simpson and James Varley, and mortar containing bullock's blood is supposed to have been used for extra strength in thin layers! The joints between the plates are reputed to have been rendered with Welsh flannel soaked in syrup and boiled for some time; certainly both kinds of join are still in excellent condition.*

37. (opposite) PONTCYSYLLTE FROM WATER LEVEL. *As one sails across the aqueduct, it is acutely obvious that all that separates oneself and one's boat from the river 127 ft below is the two-inch thickness of cast iron which forms the top of the iron trough. The tow path is cantilevered out over the water; this reduces the resistance of the water to the passage of the boat. The hexagon bolts visible in the photograph are modern reinforcement; originally there was a row of holes intended for a railing to match that of the towpath, but money was short and it was never installed.*

38. (this page) WELSH FRANKTON STAIRCASE LOCKS (118/SJ 369317–3 miles south-west of Ellesmere). *The original line of the Ellesmere Canal finished at Weston Lullingfields, north of Shrewsbury; this would have isolated the canal and the associated Montgomeryshire Canal from all the rest of the canal system, and accordingly a branch was cut from Welsh Frankton via Ellesmere and Whitchurch to join the Chester Canal near Nantwich. The staircase locks at Frankton are now long derelict, but still impressive in size and construction.*

39. BEESTON IRON LOCK (109/SJ 557597–2 miles south of Tarporley). *The Chester Canal was the link between the two parts of the Ellesmere–that from Llangollen to Nantwich, and that from Ellesmere Port on the Mersey to Chester itself. The locks at Beeston had long given trouble, for they were built on quicksand. In a characteristically inspired solution to this problem, Telford built the chamber entirely of cast iron plates bolted together like those at Chirk.*

40

40. ELLESMERE PORT WAREHOUSES (109/SJ 405773, in Ellesmere Port docks). *These famous warehouses are now unhappily almost entirely destroyed by fire. They represent Telford's approach to cargo handling at the peak of its early-nineteenth-century efficiency.* (Photograph by Courtesy of Neil Cossons).

Scottish Roads and Bridges

In 1801 Telford was asked to survey and report on communications in the Scottish Highlands, and in the next eighteen years he built 920 miles of roads and rebuilt over 280 miles of military roads. Over 1000 new bridges were made, from the smallest culverts to the impressive bridges at Craigellachie and Dunkeld. He built roads north-west from the Great Glen to link with Skye along a number of valleys; no road of any kind had existed there before this time.

41. FASSFERN BRIDGE–THE ROAD TO THE ISLES (35/NN 021789–6 miles north-west of Fort William). *This bridge is typical of the small ones erected by the hundred during the 18 years' work in the Highlands. The road was built 1803–06.*

42. THE ROAD BY LOCH GARRY (36/NH 265025–north shore of Loch Garry). *The first road to be constructed was the road to the Isles, from Fort William to Arisaig. North of this two others were driven westwards; the road in this picture is one of them, from Loch Oich to Loch Hourn through Glen Garry, in 1803–13. It was only replaced in the mid-1960s, and it is easy to find stretches of Telford's original alignment. The main difference, besides the width, is that Telford took his road up and round obstacles, while the modern engineers blasted their way through them.*

The road-construction programme was organised into six divisions, each with its own resident superintendent. John Mitchell was in overall command, as Telford's direct deputy; he covered about 10,000 miles each year on foot or horseback whatever the weather. Such was the lot of the men who built these roads.

43. (opposite: above) ROAD BY LOCH CLUANIE (36/NH 170105–north shore of Loch Cluanie). *This was the third road driven from the Great Glen towards the Sound of Sleat in 1805–12, from Loch Ness through Glen Morriston and Glen Shiel to the Kyle of Lochalsh for the short crossing to Skye. In places, as shown in the photograph, the road has been replaced in such a way that it is possible to see a section through Telford's original road.*

44. (opposite: below left) *This original road has been overlaid with tarmac, but this apart, it seems identical with the specifications laid down by Telford.*

45. (opposite: below right) *For comparison, a model section from the Science Museum in London shows a large layer of stones as foundation, obviously not needed in the actual road if there was a solid rock floor present. Two layers of smaller stones are present, with crushed material binding the whole together.*

46. (this page) TABLET ON BONAR BRIDGE (22/NH 610915–at the north end of the bridge). *Telford's original bridge here was swept away late in the nineteenth century. The cast iron spans were identical with those of Craigellachie bridge, and cast at Plas Kynaston to be delivered by canal and sea. The airy design gave minimum resistance to flood, and the spans of 50, 60, and 150 ft gave one of the very few asymmetrical bridges ever designed by Telford–necessitated here by the lack of firm foundations.*

TRAVELLER!
STOP and *Read* with GRATITUDE
The names of the PARLIAMENTARY COMMISSIONERS
appointed in the Year 1803. to direct the making
of above Five Hundred miles of Roads through
the Highlands of Scotland and of numerous
Bridges particularly those at BEAULY
SCUDDEL. BONAR. FLEET and HELMSDALE
connecting those Roads: VIZ.

RIGHT HONOURABLE CHARLES ABBOT
RIGHT HONOURABLE NICHOLAS VANSITTART
RIGHT HONOURABLE WILLIAM DUNDAS
SIR WILLIAM PULTENEY BART
ISAAC HAWKINS BROWN ESQR
CHARLES GRANT ESQR
WILLIAM SMITH ESQR
to whom were afterwards added
ARCHIBALD COLQUHON ESQR LORD ADVOCATE
CHARLES DUNDAS ESQR
RIGHT HONOURABLE NATHANIEL BOND
This BUILDING was begun Sept! 1 11.
and finished Novr 1812.
THOMAS TELFORD Architect SIMPSON & CARGIL Builders
This STONE was placed here by
GEORGE DEMPSTER of Dunnichen.
In the Year 1815.

47. (this page) GLENSHIEL BRIDGE (35/NG 990132–5 miles south-east of Shiel Bridge). *Telford followed the plan of taking the road along the side of the hill by a masonry-supported embankment and making a right-angle turn across this bridge. This followed the line of the earlier military road, and the bridge was remade, probably on the site of an earlier one, in 1814–17.*

48. (opposite: above) THE ROAD TO KINLOCH HOURN (camera position 36/NH 203035–on A87–12 miles west of Fort Augustus). *This view shows the country surveyed by Telford for his Highland roads, with the road through Glen Garry. The mountains in the distance are lost in mist, and it says much for Telford's constitution that he could stand 18 years of such work in such conditions.*

49. (opposite: below) ACHNASHEEN–THE STROMEFERRY ROAD (27/NH 158585–in Achnasheen). *The road from Dingwall struck westwards through Achnasheen from Strath Bran and on to Loch Carron and Stromeferry, then north to Loch Torridon. In the picture the original road is in front of the camera and crossing its bridge, while later roads go to Gairloch via Loch Maree. Almost all the length of the road from Dingwall to Stromeferry is original Telford, and is only now starting to be replaced after almost 180 years of use, dating from 1812–18.*

46

50. (opposite: above) CONON BRIDGE ABUTMENTS (27/NH 540559–3 miles south of Dingwall). *All that remain of this bridge are the western abutment and some parapet walling, plus the two-storey toll house in so typical a Telford design. The bridge was built between 1806 and 1809 and had spans of 45, 55, 65, 55 and 45 ft. It was replaced only when it was necessary to move very heavy loads for the power station at Dounreay. Apart from this bridge and that at Bonar, all Telford's other bridges in Scotland remain intact.*

51. (opposite: below) THE MOUND, FLEET (camera position 22/NH 767976–5 miles north of Dornoch). *From Dingwall, Telford's road went north to Bonar Bridge where it forked. One branch went to Tongue, the other north-east to Wick and Thurso. This latter road was carried across the head of Loch Fleet by the magnificent embankment shown in this picture, built between 1813 and 1816. Telford had become a master of earthworks by this time.*

52. (this page) CRAIGELLACHIE BRIDGE (29/NJ 285452–12 miles south of Elgin). *This bridge was built 1812–15, and has a span of 150 ft. The graceful cast iron members are of exactly the same appearance as those of the original Bonar Bridge, and were cast at Plas Kynaston at the same time. The bridge was erected by William Stuttle, Hazeldine's foreman. The restrained use of the material to give a graceful and airy appearance is most notable.*

In all his building works very few lives were lost, as Telford spent much time in making sure that the workmen behaved properly and in planning the constructional work to minimise danger. In addition to the many roads and bridges built in the Highlands and Islands, Telford designed a basic plan for new churches and manses in remote areas. They represent virtually his last purely architectural works and are of severe design; this was at least partly due to the fact that manse and church together must not cost more than £1,500–including all materials and transport as well as the cost of building. A number of these churches survive on the Islands.

53. BALLATER BRIDGE (42/NO 373956–32 miles west of Aberdeen). *Built 1807–9, the spans are 34, 55, 60, 55, 34 ft. A good example of masonry construction may be inspected when the river is low as here, right under the arches. The hollow wall technique was used in constructing the spandrels of the arches, thus reducing weight on the piers while maintaining the strength.*

54.   FERNESS BRIDGE (29/NH 960462–9 miles south-east of Nairn).
This bridge, with spans of 36, 55 and 36 ft, was built 1814–17 across the river Findhorn. The construction details are similar to those of Ballater bridge.

51

Elevation

Scale of Feet

Plan of Abutment below the Arch Springer

Plan of Pier

Plan of Spandrel Walls

Plan showing the Corbels on the top of the Spandrel Walls

Footpath

Carriage Way

Footpath

Spandrel Covers

Elevation

Longitudinal Section

Transverse Section

REFERENCE

Span of Four Main Arches, each	90 feet
Rise of D° D° D°	30
Span of Four Upper Arches, each	36
Rise of D° D° D°	16 feet 6 inches
Height of Roadway above the River Bed	106 feet

REFERENCE.

Width across the Soffit of Main Arches	34 feet
Projection of Upper Arches from the face of Spandrels of Lower Arches	3 feet
Total width between the Parapets	39
Thickness of each of the Piers	12

Level of Ordinary Floods.

Plan   of   the   Roadway   of   the   Framing   of   the   Foundation

55. (opposite: above) DEAN BRIDGE, EDINBURGH, *from the* Atlas. *One of the last (1829–31) and greatest stone bridges by Telford is the one still standing and in use over the Water of Leith–Dean Bridge. The arches are of unusual design, each of 90 ft span, and with maximum height of 106 ft above the water. The main arches carry the roadway, and rise 30 ft, but the footpath is carried on different arches which rise only 20 ft; the effect nowadays is to make one wonder if the bridge has been widened after building! The effect, also, is one of lightness. The drawing shows the centring used for the construction of the arches, and also the hollowness of the piers.*

56. (opposite: below) LAGGAN KIRK TIMBER BRIDGE, *from the* Atlas. *Telford was not a timber user and this bridge, now replaced, is a very unusual example of his bridge construction using this material. Its bracing is such as to give the necessary stiffness to an elastic material, and its economy in construction must have made it attractive on that score.*

57. (this page) EASTERFEARN BRIDGE (22/NH 629876–5 miles south of Bonar Bridge). *The road surveyed by Telford north from Dingwall went straight across the hills of Easter Ross; the later route goes a much longer way round the coast. The direct route has steeper gradients and a few finely situated bridges, such as this one across Easter Fearn Burn, built 1810–15.*

58. (this page) CARTLAND CRAGS BRIDGE (61/NS 868445–1 mile west of Lanark). *The drawing from Telford's* Atlas *shows how the centring timbers were arranged for the construction of the arches (1821–22) on their piers 129 ft above the Mouse Water. This bridge is possibly the most impressive in all Scotland–if one sees it from below–for it is hardly noticeable if one merely speeds across it. The finished bridge shows no sign, of course, of how it was constructed; the drawing shown here has been included to indicate something of the effort and skill required in the building of such masonry bridges.*

59. (opposite) *When seen from below, the piers rising from the water are at least as impressive as those of Pontcysyllte, while the arches still have their original masonry intact although a separate footway has been added at the side to widen the roadway. This bridge is on a road running through the Lowlands county of Lanark, to connect Falkirk with Carlisle for cattle marketing. A number of toll houses of obvious Telford design exist along this road, including one at the bridge itself–a favourite site making them difficult to avoid!*

54

Northern Harbours and Canals

Telford, in his capacity as engineer to the British Fisheries Society, had designed a number of Scottish harbours and improved others originally constructed by engineers such as Smeaton and Rennie. It is often difficult to decide exactly what Telford designed and what he merely improved. It is clear that he worked on important improvements at Aberdeen, Banff, Cullen, Dundee, Fortrose, Frazerburgh, Kirkwall and Peterhead, among other lesser works.

60. ABERDEEN HARBOUR (camera position 40/NJ 962057–by the golf course). *Telford extended and rebuilt the earlier breakwater seen across the channel in the photograph, and made other significant improvements.*

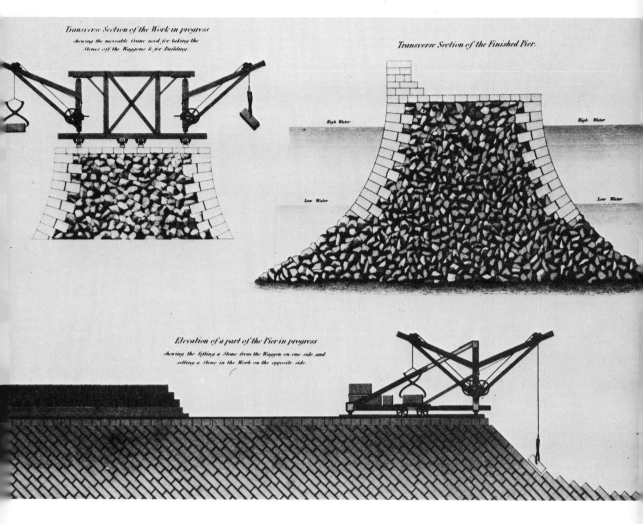

Transverse Section of the Work in progress
shewing the moveable Crane used for taking the
Stones off the Waggons & for Building.

Transverse Section of the Finished Pier.

Elevation of a part of the Pier in progress
shewing the lifting a Stone from the Waggon on one side and
setting a Stone in the Work on the opposite side.

61. *This drawing from Telford's* Atlas *shows something of the constructional methods employed at Aberdeen. The cranes were quite advanced for their time, although still relying on strong arm-power for lifting even the heaviest blocks. The arrangement of the masonry courses so as to resist the wave action in the best possible manner is plainly seen. Telford worked on improvements to Aberdeen harbour for many years, interspersed with pauses while more funds were found. He was adviser from 1801 until his death. The first phase of improvements (1809–18) was the extension of Smeaton's pier and construction of the south breakwater. The second phase (1829–34) included making a new channel for the Dee, new wet docks and quays and extensive dredging.*

62. CULLEN HARBOUR (camera position 30/NJ 511674–on the headland). *Between 1817 and 1819, Telford built the pier 250 ft long, seen on the left of the photograph, with the return pier and the projecting pier to prevent accumulation of sand. The development of the harbour, although not a large work by Telford's standards, was of the greatest importance to the local fishermen, for it afforded safe refuge and made possible exploitation of the rich fishing grounds of the northern seas. This smaller work is typical of many carried out at this time – plans of them are to be found in the Atlas.*

58

63. BANFF HARBOUR (30/NJ 689647–by the hospital, south of Meavie Point). *Telford worked at Banff from 1806 to 1823, but the main work was carried out between 1814–9. The earlier small harbour was better protected by the large stone pier seen in the distance in the photograph. Here also the construction of the harbour made an immense difference to the local fishermen.*

Small works such as improvements to ferry piers and jetties, extensions to earlier harbours, and general strengthening operations were carried out by Telford all over Scotland. Major works, in addition to those at Aberdeen, are still to be seen at Dundee. Here the graving dock still in use (265 ft long) was designed by Telford, as was Earl Grey's dock and other features. Telford was consulting engineer between 1814 and 1830.

The Caledonian Canal was an engineering triumph but a commercial failure. Its construction occupied the years between 1803 and 1822 and the government of the day proved a capricious taskmaster. There was much opposition from the landowners, but a by-product of the constructional work was that the native labourers were trained and became skilled men–a bonus compared with their normal way of life at that time.

New problems occurred frequently and the magnitude of the works was such that fresh techniques were needed. For example, two steam bucket dredgers were used for the first time on Loch Oich.

Basically, the need was to join a series of lakes by means of a relatively short total distance of canal. The sea voyage round the north of Scotland was dangerous and could be very lengthy, and the Napoleonic wars provided added incentive for a safe northern route for warships. Unfortunately, the development of steam propulsion and increase in size of vessel made the canal largely redundant, although it is still occasionally used by fishing vessels, and more frequently by pleasure craft.

64. AERIAL VIEW OF THE GREAT GLEN (taken from above Banavie. The lock staircase in the foreground is 'Neptune's Staircase', at 35/NN 114771–2 miles north-west of Fort William). *The flight of eight locks is still an outstanding engineering feature of the canal, made more impressive still by the much larger size compared with locks on contemporary British canals. The Caledonian Canal locks are 170 ft by 40 ft. In the photograph the canal enters the picture bottom left, from the sea lock at Corpach, since rather modified. The chamber was cut from the solid rock and required a large Boulton & Watt engine to keep it clear of water while work continued. Following the flight of locks, the canal is seen in its full width of 100 ft (20 ft deep), along the river Lochy's course from Loch Lochy in the middle distance. In the remote distance is Loch Oich. This aerial view shows well the nature of the difficulties facing Telford. The magnitude of his achievements is very obvious today, when one can round a bend in the road in the remote Highlands and come face to face with an ocean-going vessel!* (Photograph by courtesy of Aerofilms Ltd)

65. THE CANAL NEAR GAIRLOCHY (camera position 35/NN 146816–2 miles south of Gairlochy). *The width of the navigation is obvious in this view of part of the western section. Much care was needed on this section to control the water sweeping down the mountains after snow or heavy rain, and among other measures three sluices divert water into the river Lochy 25 ft below– a spectacular sight when in action. The large size of the earthworks is not obvious until one stands beneath them (see next picture), when it is apparent that the amount of earthmoving involved was at least as great as much subsequent railway construction required. Because of the remoteness of the canal, Telford's works here never drew the attention and respect that rather smaller works commanded in the south. The whole canal is well worth visiting as an object lesson for those who believe that it was the advent of railway construction which compelled engineers to work on massive scale.*

62

66. THE LOY AQUEDUCT (35/NN 149818–2 miles south of Gairlochy). *The river Loy is a tributary of the Lochy, and the canal is carried over it by a substantial aqueduct shown in the photograph. The width of the canal necessitates a much wider aqueduct than one sees on normal canals. A saw mill was built nearby–some remains still exist–and accommodation roads were taken under the canal here also. The stone was quarried largely at Banavie, with granite facings from another quarry at Loch Linnhe near Ballachulish.*

67. LAGGAN CUTTING (camera position 36/NN 286965–near Laggan locks). *This very impressive summit cutting is larger in scale than almost all railway works and should be sailed through to appreciate its size. Plateways and barrow runs were used in its digging and, as soon as it could be flooded, each part of the excavation was deepened by the dredging machines from Loch Oich. The trees were originally planted to bind together the sides; nowadays they mask the size of the work. The steam dredging engines were constructed at Butterley ironworks to the designs of Bryan Donkin. The first was put into service in 1816, the second two years later. Each could lift 800 tons per day, and this was necessary in Loch Oich for it was very shallow. Even when the canal was opened throughout in October 1822 the channel through this loch was only 12 ft deep, instead of the 20 ft originally specified.*

64

68.   CLACHNAHARRY SEA LOCK (28/NH 645468–2 miles north-west of Inverness). *The shore of Beauly Firth shelves gradually; therefore the entrance lock had to be sited 400 yds from shore so that it could be entered at any state of tide. 55 ft of mud was present on top of a hard bottom; piles could not be driven and a coffer-dam could not be constructed. The solution was to build out from the shore a great clay embankment, shown in the photograph. Where the lock was to be built, this clay was weighted with stones; it settled, squeezing out the mud from beneath. After six months, this allowed a coffer dam to be built, but a steam engine was constantly at work to keep the workings from flooding. A thick floor and six-foot thick masonry walls were installed to complete a work of the greatest difficulty, which remains in good order still. The result is not spectacular nowadays, but it remains an impressive achievement to have built the then largest lock in the world in the middle of a sea of mud.*

The Gotha Canal

In 1808 Telford was invited by King Gustav Adolf of Sweden to work on surveying and constructing a ship canal from the North Sea to the Baltic. A waterway across Sweden was an old idea; a chain of lakes might be interlinked to connect the two, to bring strategic and commercial advantage. The westernmost part of such a link had been completed in 1800 as the Trollhätte canal; this had spurred on Count von Platen to work assiduously to revive the scheme for its completion. The Count and Telford were to become close friends over the years. 114 miles of route were surveyed that same year and plans drawn up before Telford returned to England.

The plans were for a waterway 82 ft wide at surface by 10 ft deep, with locks to pass vessels 105 ft by 23 ft. There were already 52 miles of navigation existing in the western section; a further 53 miles of canal would link 133 miles of lake navigation, to give a total length of 238 miles sea to sea. A work of considerable magnitude indeed!

The summit level was 278 ft above sea-level, in a large cutting through granite. To drop the canal into Berg, Telford planned 15 locks, including four pairs and a staircase of 7. All this was approved in 1809 and work commenced at once.

Although von Platen had at his command a force of no less than 60,000 soldiers and seamen, they were totally inexperienced and badly needed a force of skilled men from England to act as leaven. Specimens of suitable tools were also needed. All of these were provided, together with many plans and drawings with attendant specifications. Telford was accorded a Swedish knighthood, but remained plain Mr Telford

66

except when addressed by communications from Sweden; he stated that he preferred to be known by performance of useful works than by enjoyment of splendid orders.

A series of minor difficulties was overcome, some of them occasioned by the personalities of those sent out to supervise the work; Telford makes plain that he himself turned a blind eye at times!

By 1817 an iron foundry was started for the production of the various parts needed and in 1819 a pair of iron lock gates weighing 48 tons were sent from Hazeldine & Thomson's foundry at Broseley in Shropshire, to be imitated in Sweden.

In 1822 a steam dredger was shipped out, on Telford's recommendation following the success of his dredgers on the Caledonian Canal. That same year von Platen visited Telford in England and the western part of the canal was opened on 23 September.

Further difficulties, especially with shallowness in one of the lakes, were overcome, but von Platen died in 1829 without seeing his navigation fully opened. This was achieved in 1832, after 22 years of effort involving the expenditure of 100 million man-hours!

Many details of design, especially of lock furniture, are similar to those of the Caledonian Canal; the Gotha remains much as it was when built, although it does have some commercial traffic in the summer months.

69. DETAILS OF LOCK CONSTRUCTION ON THE GOTHA CANAL. *This drawing, from Telford's* Atlas, *shows a staircase pair of locks and details of both timber and iron gates.*

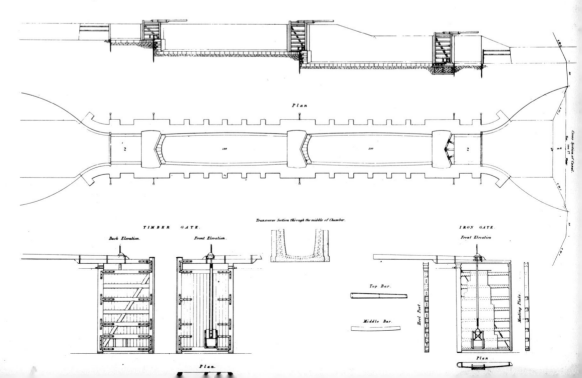

The Holyhead Road

At the same time as help was being sought for the Scottish Highlands, Irish MPs were pressing their own case for improved communications between London and Dublin. Holyhead was chosen as the sea port for this and harbour works were put in hand. Nothing, however, was done about the roads between London and Holyhead; Rennie, who advised about the harbour works, considered that an engineer did not concern himself with mere roads.

Twenty-four turnpike trusts were responsible for this road, and the further west one went, the worse was the upkeep. In 1808 the Post Office tried to extend the mail coach service to Holyhead, but in vain. At this juncture, Telford was appointed to examine the route between Shrewsbury and Holyhead; he had no reservations about road building!

A report was issued in 1811 but no action was taken until 1815 when a Commission was set up, with Telford surveying the whole route from London to Holyhead. This survey was completed by March 1817 and work went on from then for the next fifteen years–although coaches could use parts of the road long before that time.

Telford's roads are few in England; they used massive foundations and were costly, but they certainly lasted. Many are still in use–much of the present A5 Holyhead Road is on the original alignment, albeit with different surface. Some curves have been altered, and many parking areas have been made from the original Telford construction in such places; a little digging shows clearly the method of building.

Work was begun west of Llangollen and by 1819 coaches could run to Bangor. Beyond there, the major obstacle was the crossing of the Menai

Straits. Here was a ferry crossing to daunt the bravest; only in the fairest weather could coaches be conveyed. Many plans had been prepared for this crossing long before Telford came on the scene; all had been defeated by the Admiralty's insistence that vessels of the largest size should be able to pass the Straits, and without any interruption to navigation while it was built!

70. MENAI BRIDGE (106/SH 557713–1½ miles south-west of Bangor). *This view shows the bridge from the mainland side, with masonry arches, cables and towers, and Telford's original iron fencing still in place.*

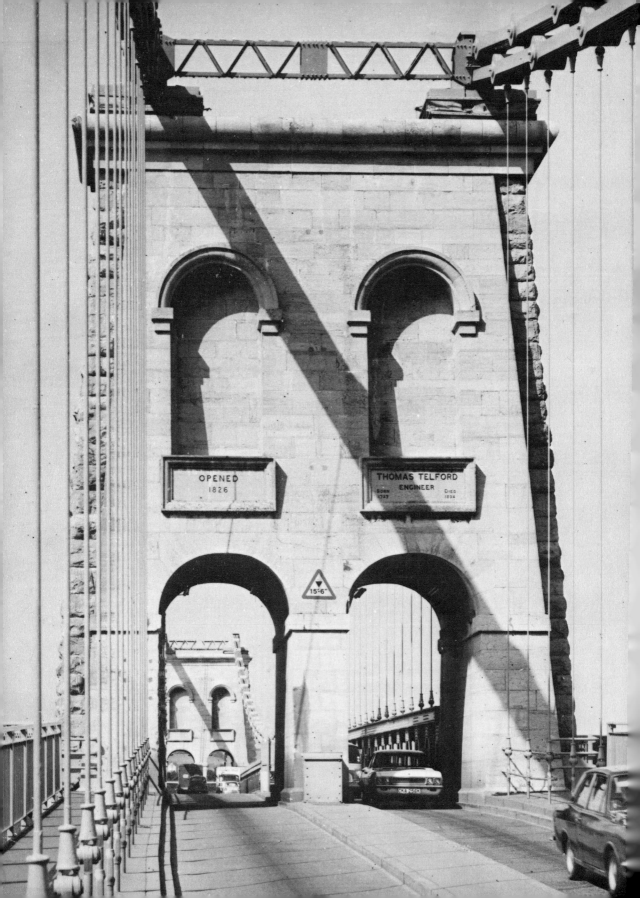

OPENED
1826

THOMAS TELFORD
ENGINEER

BORN
1757

DIED
1834

15'6"

The design of the bridge took into account the erection without impeding navigation. The arches are of span 52 ft 6 in and the towers are 153 ft high to give a suspended span of 579 ft and headway of 100 ft. The chains were assembled and fixed to their underground anchorages by early 1825, when all the masonry was completed. On 26 April 1825 Telford personally supervised the raising of the first chain. This was laid on a raft to be pulled under the bridge, to be attached to the landward side chain dangling from its tower almost to high water mark; the Anglesey chain was at the top of the Pig Island tower. The intermediate section was pinned into place by raising the end with capstans operated from the Anglesey shore, in a total of 2 hours 20 minutes. The other fifteen chains were raised in a similar manner whenever the weather was suitable, the sixteenth being placed on 9 July. The building of the suspended roadway platforms was thereafter straightforward.

71. MENAI BRIDGE TOWER. *The arrangement of the cables is shown, with the suspension system. The flat link cables are not the originals, for these were replaced about twenty years ago; the appearance is identical however. Before using such cables, Telford carried out a series of experiments using a special Bramah hydraulic press to determine the sections required for a particular strength. The links were a little over nine feet long, of malleable iron, and were made by William Hazeldine at Upton Forge near Shrewsbury. Each link was tested to a safety margin of 100% on a special tensile-testing machine in Shrewsbury, and was protected from corrosion by being plunged into a bath of linseed oil while hot, and then stove-dried. An innovation for drilling the holes accurately was to use what we would nowadays call a jig.*

72.   MENAI BRIDGE FROM ANGLESEY (camera position 106/SH 545718–1 mile east of Llanfair). *The grace of the bridge is seen in this classic view, with the mountains in the background and the waters of the strait in front.*

The opening of the bridge, so major a piece of work, was remarkable. After midnight on 30 January 1826, the Royal Mail came down the Nant Ffrancon pass, with only its normal passenger complement. A few connected with the bridge clambered aboard at Bangor and Bangor Ferry Inn and at 1.35 am on that morning the first coach went across the bridge. Telford was not among them; he didn't cross until daylight, on his way to Shrewsbury. He was at that time 69 years of age.

73.   THE BLOCKS USED TO HOIST THE MENAI CABLES *(from the* Atlas*). The considerable attention to detail paid by Telford to all such matters was a major factor in the remarkable freedom from death and injury which was so characteristic of his works. In the drawing, the cable end is almost drawn to the link awaiting it.*

Fig. 1.

Elevation

Fig. 2.

Plan

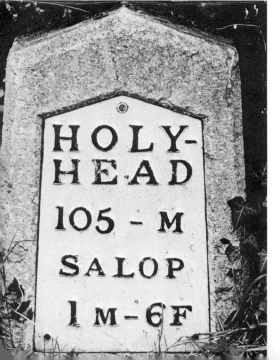

HOLY-
HEAD
105 - M
SALOP
1M - 6F

74. (above) PULLEY BLOCKS ACTUALLY USED IN THE BUILDING (to be seen in the house covering the ends of the cables at the mainland side). *Still preserved in good condition are examples of the actual pulley blocks used in 1825 to hoist the cables into position. Both single- and treble-sheeved blocks are present, as shown in use in the drawing above.*

75. (left) HOLYHEAD ROAD MILEPOST (118/SJ 468133–1½ miles out of Shrewsbury, at end of by-pass). *Telford designed every detail of the road, including its furniture. This is an original milepost, of granite with inset cast iron plate, of the kind which is still commonplace along almost the entire length of the present A5 Holyhead Road.*

76. TELFORD TOLL HOUSE (118/SJ 619106–Burcot, 3 miles west of Wellington). *This is a standard Holyhead Road tollhouse, another Telford detail design. The original entrance was in front of the bay, where there is a window now. A number of such tollhouses are to be found along the present A5 Road.*

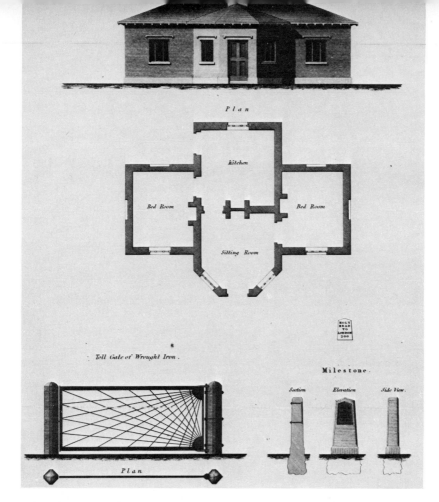

Plan

kitchen

Bed Room

Bed Room

Sitting Room

Toll Gate of Wrought Iron.

Milestone.

Section   Elevation   Side View.

Plan

77. (this page) A PAGE FROM TELFORD'S *ATLAS showing his detail designs for various parts of his Holyhead Road. The standard plan for a tollhouse is shown and matches the surviving examples. The standard milestone design and tollgate design are recognisable from many surviving examples.*

78. (opposite: above) TWO-STOREY TOLLHOUSE (106/SH 532716–on A5 in Llanfair). *The two-storey tollhouse is rather less common than the single, but there are several on Anglesey and another at Montford Bridge. This Llanfair example is unique in having its toll boards still in place.*

79. (opposite: below) TELFORD TOLL GATE (117/SJ 054437– opposite the entrance to Rug castle, 1½ miles west of Corwen). *Telford's original toll gates are now scarce, although several are well-preserved at the mainland side of the Menai Bridge.*

80. THE WATERLOO BRIDGE (107/SH 799557–at the south side of Bettwys-y-coed). *The Holyhead road crosses the river Conway by this bridge, built–as it says on it–in the year the battle of Waterloo was fought–1815. The span is decorated with cast emblems of the four nations–the rose, the leek, the thistle and the shamrock. It is quite an extravagant example of iron founding and rare in Telford's usually rather austere designs. The bridge carries a reminder that it was cast by William Hazeldine (at Plas Kynaston) and erected by William Stuttle. Stuttle was Hazeldine's foreman, responsible for putting together most of the cast iron structures cast by Hazeldine for Telford, but it is only here that he is commemorated.*

78

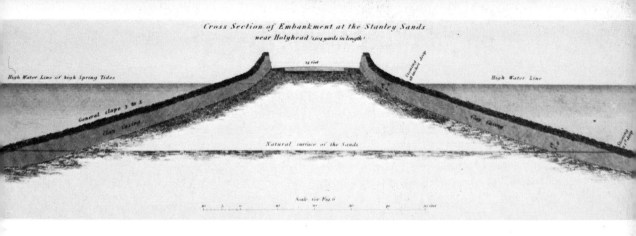

High Water Line of high Spring Tides

High Water Line

24 feet

General Masonry Slope

General slope 3 to 1

Hand Casing

Rag Casing

Natural surface of the Sands

Scale for Fig. 6

81. THE STANLEY EMBANKMENT (from Telford's *Atlas*). *The considerable earthworks necessary to build this embankment are shown in this section.*

82. THE STANLEY EMBANKMENT (camera position 106/SH 285798–2½ miles south-east of Holyhead). *The old road detoured at Valley to take advantage of the four-mile bridge at the narrowest crossing to Holyhead Island. Telford took a direct route across the Stanley Sands by means of a great embankment 1300 yds long, 16 ft high and 114 ft wide at base. It was built within a year, opened in 1823 and is still in use as part of the A5. The photograph shows the rubble walling which protects the roadway against storm damage.*

83. THE NANTFFRANCON PASS–LOOKING DOWN (camera position 107/SH 648606–just below Ogwen Cottage). *Telford decided that there must be no gradient steeper than 1 in 20 and in the mountainous country between Llangollen and Bangor this was no mean requirement. Deep cuttings had to be blasted and large embankments made, and high retaining walls were commonplace. The most impressive part of the route where the gradient never exceeds 1 in 22 is the road out of Capel Curig, by the foot of Tryfan and down the Nant Ffrancon pass by Ogwen Cottage. In this photograph the road is followed down the valley, supported by the considerable retaining wall and protected on the hill-side by a screening wall against rock falls. The roadway is the original width, even though it carries traffic in quantity undreamt of in 1820. Set into the far wall is a milepost of characteristic form.*

84. THE NANTFFRANCON PASS – LOOKING UP (camera position a few yards nearer Ogwen Cottage than for the facing picture). *The gradient of this road is such as to enable the motorist to speed up the pass in top gear, crossing this bridge over the Ogwen without even noticing it. Just to the left of the picture is a cutting blasted out of solid rock and protected from rock falls by further revetments. In front is the Cottage at Ogwen–mecca for rock climbers– and behind that the precipitous mass of Tryfan. And through all this the road goes on a top-gear gradient. It is a pity in a way that it should be so, for many a motorist could with advantage pause here to survey the scene and recollect that this road was laid out for him by Telford before 1820.*

85, 86, 87. CONWAY BRIDGE (107/SH 785775–in Conway). *Picture 85 (above) is a general view. Picture 86 (left) is a close view of the chains. Picture 87 (opposite) is a view of the toll house.*

Conway Bridge is not part of the Holyhead Road but is on a separate road from Chester to Bangor, where it joins the Holyhead Road. Conway Bridge has a span of 327 ft between towers and ranks as a major work in its own right, even though overshadowed by the larger bridge at Menai. It is a rare example of Telford's departure from the purely functional style of most of his bridge work. In deference to the adjacency of Conway Castle, the towers were designed to resemble castellated gateways and the toll house was also designed to blend in with the mediaeval surroundings. The approach embankment, 2015 ft long by 300 ft wide at base, is also impressive in its own right and was the heaviest part of the work. Some of the ropes from Menai were used to suspend a timber platform on which the cables were assembled, the swiftness of the current precluding use of a raft for assembly. The links in this bridge are the original ones installed by Telford and they are still in good order. The bridge was opened on 1 July 1826, about half-past midnight, by the Chester Mail which carried as many passengers as could find a hold!

Severn Bridges

88.   BEWDLEY BRIDGE (130/SO 787754–4 miles west of Kidder-minster). *Telford built a number of bridges along the Severn, but of the one at Bewdley he was especially proud. Built in 1798, it was completed in one season –albeit an exceptionally dry one. The stone came from Arley quarry, only four miles upstream and the total cost was £9,000. This bridge is still in good order and is possibly the best example of Telford's early stone work. The architectural merit of this bridge is high, perhaps because it was designed before Telford had quite forgotten his aspirations to become an architect.*

89. HOLT FLEET BRIDGE (130/SO 824634–6 miles north of Worcester). *Built in 1827, this bridge remains a good example of Telford's economical application of cast iron to bridge building. The stone abutments have the characteristic appearance of his masonry designs and his respect for the force of Severn floods is shown in the great unobstructed span over the water.*

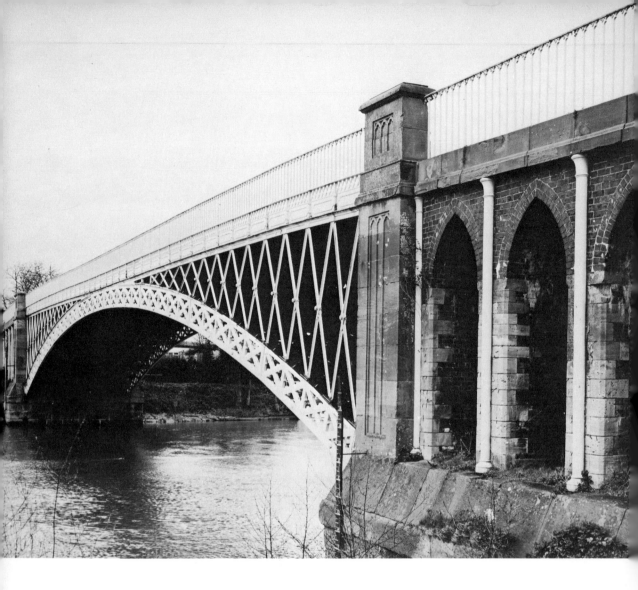

90. MYTHE BRIDGE (143/SO 889337–1 mile north of Tewkesbury).
*Designed in 1823, the bridge was completed in 1826. The single iron span is
170 ft long, with a masonry abutment on this side–the east–pierced for flood
waters. The iron was cast by William Hazeldine and the original metalwork is
intact. There is a small toll house on the eastern approach, also intact and of
rather nice design in character with the whole. This is a fine example of Telford's
iron bridge work.*

86

91. OVER BRIDGE (143/SO 817196–1 mile west of Gloucester). *This is of unusual design, based on an earlier bridge by Perronet for the Seine at Neuilly. The special appearance is due to the body of the arch being an ellipse with a chord line of 150 ft and a rise of 35 ft, while the external arch stones were set on the same chord with a rise of only 13 ft. This gives the funnel-shaped appearance of the arch, most apparent at the springing and less so at the crown, and calculated to present minimum resistance to flood waters. The stone came from the same quarries at Arley as that for Bewdley bridge 27 years before. The foundations for the abutment walls were not as sound as might have been, for when the centring was eased the crown of the arch dropped ten inches. Notwithstanding, the bridge stands to this day, the scaffolding in the picture being in place for periodic pointing.*

St Katharine's Dock

92. *In 1824 the St Katharine's Dock Company was formed to build a new 'free' dock on a site next to the Tower of London. In the 27 acres no fewer than 1250 dwellings were demolished to make way for the works, with Telford as engineer. Work commenced in May 1826, just after the Menai Bridge was finished. The awkward shape of the site and the need for maximum warehousing and wharfage left only ten acres for water; this precluded the usual rectangular basins and the plate below, taken from Telford's* Atlas, *shows how the engineer made excellent use of the site.*

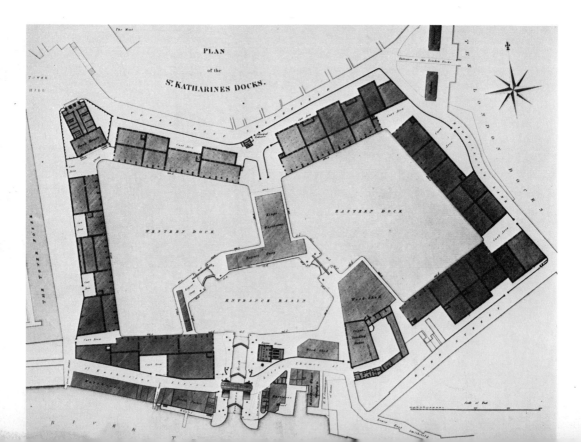

93. ST KATHARINE'S DOCK (160/TQ 340805–by the side of Tower Bridge). *This view is from the site of Telford's Wood Shed, now covered by a warehouse of 1852, looking across the entrance basin to the export quay with the King's warehouse behind. Between the pillars the entrance to the western dock is visible, with its warehouses forming the background on the left of the picture. The Dock Company's architect who collaborated with Telford in the design of the warehouses was Philip Hardwick, later to gain fame as the designer of the Euston portico. The docks were opened complete on 25 October 1828, only two and a half years from the laying of the foundation stone.*

94. THE DOCK ENTRANCE *is well seen from Tower Bridge. The house next to the lock is Telford's original Dock Master's Office and the appearance of the entrance lock is little changed from the original. In the background on the left is the dock wall and behind it the site of the engine house for opening the lock gates and pumping water. The design of the entrance basin is such that either dock could be used at will, while the other was being scoured. The lock is 180 ft long by 45 ft wide and could be filled at any state of tide in a maximum of 5½ minutes from a culvert opening in the middle of the river.*

95. DEMOLITION OF THE WAREHOUSES *fronting the river was undertaken in 1971 as part of redevelopment plans for the area. This afforded an opportunity to see something of their structure, as seen in the picture. The timber construction is a little surprising in view of the use of cast iron for such work in the preceding twenty years and more and may have been due to the collaboration between Telford and Hardwick. Something of these works will be preserved in the new scheme, so that Telford's achievements on this site need not be remembered only from pictures.*

Telford's Improvements

Telford was consulted about many improvements to existing systems; a full list would be too lengthy to give here and only a few of his more important innovations have been selected for illustration. Among the most important of all was his work on the new Harecastle tunnel.

96. HARECASTLE TUNNEL ENTRANCES (110/SJ 837542–near the centre of Kidsgrove). *The Trent & Mersey Canal was a trunk route carrying an enormous traffic, but little had been spent on improvement since Brindley constructed it. In particular the Harecastle Tunnel, although nearly 3,000 yds long, was only single width and constituted a major bottleneck. In 1820 John Rennie was called in to inspect the tunnel, was appalled at what he found and recommended its closure for repairs when a second tunnel had been constructed. Telford advised similarly in 1822, but the work was not put in hand until 1825.*

97. THE TUNNEL INTERIOR *was fitted with a towpath, very recently removed to improve navigation past the section where the roof bulges in. This was a great improvement on Brindley's tunnel, through which boats had to be legged. Inside, the other end can be seen as a pinpoint of light, so straight is the course.*

Work was started at fifteen different shafts giving thirty headings, special brickyards were built and Boulton & Watt engines were used to pump. In just over two years the tunnel was finished, lined with seven million bricks, and the whole in exact accordance with Telford's plans and without any loss of life at all.

98. DRAWINGS FROM TELFORD'S *ATLAS. These show the construction of the towing path with a cross section of the tunnel, and the centring used to support the arches while the bricks were laid.*

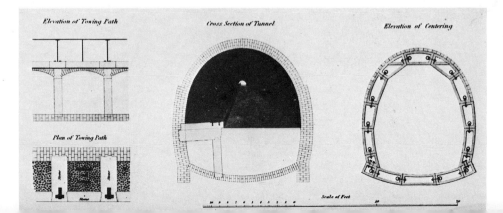

Elevation of Towing Path   Cross Section of Tunnel   Elevation of Centering

Plan of Towing Path

Scale of Feet

99. (opposite: above) THREE LEVELS OF CANAL (camera position–131/SP 019888–from the railway footbridge near Brasshouse Lane bridge). *The topmost line, long dry, is that of the Brindley's original short summit. The middle line was constructed by Smeaton in 1790, at the Wolverhampton level. The lower line is Telford's, made on the Birmingham level and requiring enormous earthmoving operations to make the cutting. The straight wide canal is a dramatic improvement.*

100. (opposite: below) GALTON BRIDGE (1829) (131/SP 015894–carries Roebuck Lane). *The cutting is 70 ft deep, the canal 40 ft wide with a towpath each side, the whole spanned by this magnificent 150 ft cast iron bridge.*

101. (below) AERIAL VIEW OF BIRMINGHAM. *The earlier Brindley contour canal is seen winding its way round the Telford line, straight and wide, showing dramatically the improvement wrought on the earlier navigation.* (Photograph by courtesy of Aerofilms Ltd).

Telford advised on many other projects. He was associated with nearly thirty canals, over fifty docks and harbours, a number of waterworks, several river navigations, surveys of over a dozen roads, and five railways, including the Liverpool & Manchester. In his capacity as engineer to the Exchequer Bill Loan Commission his duties included advising on the feasibility of the projects for which government loans were sought. In addition he carried out various investigations, for example into Parker's cement, the tensile strength of iron, the feasibility of a sewer beneath St Paul's church, and on the resistance of canal barges. All this besides the works described in more detail in this book; he was, of course, over-worked, but the strain did not tell until he was well advanced in years.

He left behind a large number of letters to various friends and his Reports on various subjects, numbering over forty, are invaluable in gaining an understanding of engineering as practised in the early part of the nineteenth century.

Before his death, he was to build one other major canal–the Birmingham & Liverpool Junction canal, now the main part of the Shropshire Union.

102. MAP OF THE NENE OUTFALL (from the *Atlas*). *Telford worked with the older Rennie on several Fens drainage schemes, the most notable being the Eau Brink Cut which turned out to be too small. With the younger Rennie's help this was widened and became completely successful. Also with the younger Rennie Telford worked on the Nene outfall, from Gunthorpe below Wisbech to Crab's Hole Sluice on the Wash. Telford alone was responsible for his last work in the Fens, the draining of the North Level, by making the New North Level Drain, 36 ft wide, from Clow's Cross to the head of the Nene Outfall channel. Started in 1830 and completed in 1834 this drain had an immediate impact on the drainage of the fenlands. All these various drainage works are shown on the map opposite, where their large scale becomes obvious.*

Map of the
NENE OUTFALL,
and part of the
DRAINAGE
dependent on it.
1838.

The Last Canal

The decision to build a new canal, to link Birmingham directly with Liverpool, was taken in 1825 with Telford as the engineer. This was a very different canal from any before; it was direct and it was built using earth-moving techniques on a grand scale. It was not to be opened until 1835 when, on 2 March, exactly six months after Telford's death, the first boat passed the full 39 miles from Autherley Junction on the Staffordshire & Worcestershire canal to the Nantwich basin on the Chester canal.

103. NORBURY JUNCTION (119/SJ 793228-10 miles west of Stafford). *When the new canal was built, a branch was made through Newport to join with the Shrewsbury canal at Wappenshall Junction. In this way Telford's first canal was joined with his last. The photograph was taken from the towpath of the Newport branch, looking through the arch of the roving bridge to the main line of the new canal.*

104. COWLEY TUNNEL (119/SJ 824197–5 miles south of Norbury Junction). *This is the only tunnel on the route and is only 81 yds long, cut from poor rock. It is one of the several major features of the southern section of the canal and caused much concern in the digging as over 600 yds of originally projected tunnel had to be opened out into cutting, so friable was the rock.*

Work started on the canal in January 1827, at Nantwich. By the time this canal came to be built the cost of procuring the land had risen enormously from that of earlier canals. An agricultural revolution had occurred in which small landholdings had been amalgamated to make the new landowner enormously powerful. One such landowner forced a diversion at the Nantwich end which resulted in considerable extra work being required, including a high bank for almost half a mile. Other major works at this end of the canal were the crossing of the Weaver at Audlem and the Tern at Market Drayton, and a deep cutting north of that town.

105. SHELMORE BANK (camera position 119/SJ 794224– ½ mile south of Norbury Junction). *A deviation was necessary here, as Lord Anson refused to allow the canal to be cut through his game preserves. Instead of making the navigation on a level, the canal had to be taken along an embankment sixty feet high for over a mile. Great difficulty was experienced in making this embankment, seen in the photograph with the road beneath. Work began in the summer of 1829, with 400 men and 70 horses. Spoil was brought from the nearby cuttings, but bad weather delayed progress, although 490,000 cubic yards of spoil had been tipped by the following July. Within a year the bank was raised to a quarter of its full height, but it was unstable and began to subside along its entire length. The marl used was unsuitable, and Telford ordered that only lighter soils be used in future. By the end of 1831 the bank was full height for much of its length and it seemed that it would be completed by late 1832, but the bank continued to sink. A great deal of it slipped away in August 1832, and early in 1833 a conference was held at Telford's house in London without a successful outcome. The bank was not completed until after Telford's death.*

100

106, 107. STRETTON AQUEDUCT (119/SJ 873108–3 miles west of Gailey roundabout). *The upper picture shows the boatman's view of the approaching aqueduct, while below is a view of the appearance of the cast iron trough from its side. The whole is largely in original condition, and Telford's aqueduct across Telford's road links the two main kinds of engineering project with which he was associated. The date is 1832 and Telford has after his name the letters showing that he was a fellow of the Royal Society and of the Royal Society of Edinburgh.*

108. TYRLEY CUTTING (camera position–119/SJ 698304–3 miles south-east of Market Drayton). *This enormous work was constructed with great difficulty, the strata of friable rock alternating with clay which was treacherous both dry and wet. Rain and frost dislodged masses of material avalanche-fashion and these slips continued for many months. The angle of the sides was reduced and slowly the vegetation took root and bound the loose material. This cutting remains to this day an extremely impressive feature of the canal system of the British Isles and its associated accommodation bridges soaring away overhead look all of their 70 ft height.*

109. TYRLEY LOCKS (camera position–119/SJ 687331–1 mile south-east of Market Drayton). *A flight of five locks takes the canal to its long summit pound. The navigation below the locks is cut from the solid rock as seen in the picture and the further cuttings follow south of the locks.*

Although work on the canal had commenced at the Nantwich end with the embankment near Henhull Lane, considerable trouble was experienced there and for the same reason as at Shelmore–earth movements. In January 1830 slips occurred which blocked the road below and this occurred again the following July after a wet summer and spring. In the following January still more spoil had to be tipped and it was not until the middle of 1832 that the bank was secure. Similar troubles occurred at other places and this series of misfortunes delayed the opening of the canal for several years.

110. AUDLEM LOCKS (camera position–119/SJ 658422–1 mile south of Audlem). *Telford arranged all the locks on the canal, with only one exception, into the northern part where the canal leaves the Cheshire Plain. The major number is concentrated around Audlem where a flight of fifteen in 1½ miles lifts the canal a total of 93 ft. The picture is taken looking down the flight from above lock 4.*

During the construction of this last canal, Telford had been in worsening health; the years of unremitting hardship and toil had begun to take effect. When the meeting to discuss Shelmore Bank was necessary in 1833, it had to take place at Telford's house in London as his health was too bad to allow him to travel. The meeting took place at the house in Abingdon Street, now no longer standing. Until 1821, when he was sixty-four, Telford had no house of his own; when he was in town he put up at the Salopian Coffee House at Charing Cross and there he met his friends and discussed his business plans. 24 Abingdon Street was directly opposite the Houses of Parliament and very handy for all the business with which he was connected.

At about this time the Institution of Civil Engineers was founded, but was slow to grow. At the beginning of 1820 Telford was invited to become its first President, and when he accepted, this set the seal on the progress of the Institution. He was keen that it should become the vehicle for propagating a common pool of knowledge to advance the profession and his influence ensured its success. The *Proceedings* began, and Telford's gifts of books and drawings laid the foundation of the excellent library. In 1828 the Royal Charter was awarded and Telford came to play a less active part in its affairs; deafness troubled him and he was forced to live more slowly. He had never married and although he had many friends none was very close. Doubtless he was concerned that Shelmore Bank had not been completed and he had had rough treatment from the directors of the Liverpool & Manchester Railway. Soon after his death England went railway mad, the canal companies paid dearly for their lack of foresight and their past greediness, and the roads were silent as traffic moved to rail. Telford's works were, for a time, forgotten. How fortunate we are that he built so well that we nowadays, with benefit of hindsight, can see his genius made evident in his surviving masterpieces.

In Memoriam

Telford, as we have said above, is remembered by his works and that is as he desired. He was buried, against his wishes, in Westminster Abbey; his fine monument is properly placed in great company. More important, his Institution flourishes and so do his contracting methods and system of stringent specification. These are more important than monuments in stone.

111. TELFORD'S MEMORIAL, WESTERKIRK (75/NY 297911 – 8 miles west of Langholm). *This memorial in his native valley, erected quite recently, reminds us that Telford for all his greatness never forgot his own Meggat Water and Eskdale. This is a memorial in less grand surroundings than Westminster Abbey, but in country where Telford is still a name remembered.*

112. LANGHOLM LIBRARY (76/NY 365845–in the centre of Langholm). *When Telford died, he left £2,000 in trust to the parishes of Langholm and Westkirk for the establishment of libraries. He had derived knowledge and solace from books and he was determined that his kinsfolk should not be denied access to books in their turn. His total estate was only £16,600. Although this was not a small sum in those days, it is relatively small for one engaged in so many enterprises of such great moment. On the other hand, it is known that for some of his work, such as that for the Fisheries Society, he accepted no fee at all; it was the challenge and not the reward which was the interest.*

107

Principal Dates

1757	9 August, born in Glendinning, Eskdale
1771	apprenticed to a stonemason in Langholm
1780(-82)	working as stonemason in Edinburgh
1782(-84)	working as stonemason in London, at Somerset House
1784(-86)	working as supervisor, Commissioner's House, Portsmouth
1787	responsible for repairs to Shrewsbury Castle
1787(-93)	responsible for Shrewsbury Gaol
1788	appointed Surveyor to the County of Salop
1790	Montford Bridge
1792	St Mary's, Bridgenorth
1793	Engineer to Ellesmere Canal (until 1805, thereafter consultant)
1794	Pontcysyllte aqueduct designed (finished 1805)
1795(-1800)	engineer to Shrewsbury Canal. Longdon aqueduct
1795(-96)	Buildwas Bridge
1796	Chirk aqueduct
1801	First Highland Survey
1802	Second Highland Survey
1803(-22)	Caledonian Canal
1803	Scottish roadbuilding started
1805(-06)	Tongland Bridge
1806	Glasgow water supply
1806(-08)	Dunkeld Bridge
1808	visit to Sweden
1809(-33)	Gotha Canal

1810(–34)	Aberdeen harbour works
1811	First report on Holyhead Road
1812(–15)	Craigellachie Bridge
1813	Second visit to Sweden
1817(–29)	Adviser to Exchequer Loan Commissioners
1819(–26)	Menai and Conway bridges
1820	First President of the Institution of Civil Engineers
1820(–25)	Surveys of Great North Road
1820(–23)	Lanarkshire roads (65 miles)
1822(–27)	Harecastle tunnel
1823(–25)	South Wales road surveys
1824(–34)	Birmingham Canal improvements
1825(–34)	Birmingham & Liverpool Junction Canal
1826	St Katharine's Dock completed
1827	Don Bridge, Aberdeen
1833	Broomielaw Bridge, Glasgow
1834	Died, 2 September. Buried in Westminster Abbey.

Further Reading

L. T. C. Rolt–THOMAS TELFORD (Longmans Green, London; 1958)
This book is very well-written, packed with accurate information, and a 'must' for anyone interested in Telford. Mr Rolt's book has been a mainstay in our selection of Telford's works to visit in our preparation for the present book.

Sir A. Gibb–THE STORY OF TELFORD (Maclehose and Co, London; 1935)
Very useful for the full list of Telford's works.

S. Smiles–LIVES OF THE ENGINEERS VOL 2 (reprinted by David & Charles, Newton Abbot; 1968. Originally published by Murray in 1862)
Smiles romanticises his subjects and his information is not always reliable. The book remains useful.

J. Rickman (ed)–THE LIFE OF THOMAS TELFORD WRITTEN BY HIMSELF (1839). ATLAS TO THE LIFE OF THOMAS TELFORD (1838)
These books are invaluable, as they tell in Telford's own words and drawings what he in retrospect thought of his works. The *Atlas* is especially valuable, but both books are very hard to come by nowadays.

R. Southey–JOURNAL OF A TOUR IN SCOTLAND IN 1819 (John Murray, London; 1929)
A vivid description of a tour with Telford.

Index